Blend Phonics Timed Fluency Drills

For Beginning and Remedial Readers

Designed to Accompany

Mrs. Hazel Loring's 1980 Phonics Masterpiece:

Reading Made Easy with Blend Phonics for First Grade

Mr. Potter's Secret of Reading:
"Look at all the Letters the Right Way,
and <u>No</u> Guessing."

DEDICATION

TO ALL MY TUTORING STUDENTS OVER THE LAST TWENTY YEARS

WHO MOTIVAGED ME TO DO MY BEST

SO THEY COULD BE A SUCCESS

CONTENTS

APPENDICES

Blend Phonics Fluency Drills

Step 1

Short Vowels & Consonants

Drills 1 – 9

Units 1 – 5

Decodable Stories 1 – 7

Phonvisual Chart Picture-Sound Correspondences

Short Vowels

-a- c<u>a</u>t, **-e-** b<u>e</u>d, **-i-** f<u>i</u>sh, **-o-** t<u>o</u>p, **-u-** d<u>u</u>ck

Single Letter Consonants & qu, ck

c-<u>k</u>ey, **d**-<u>d</u>uck, **f**-<u>f</u>an, **g**-<u>g</u>oat, **h**-<u>h</u>orn, **j**-<u>j</u>ar

k-<u>k</u>ey, **l**-<u>l</u>eaf, **m**-<u>m</u>onkey, **n**-<u>n</u>est, **p**-<u>p</u>ig, **qu**-<u>qu</u>een

r-<u>r</u>abbit, **s**-<u>s</u>aw, **t**-<u>t</u>op, **v**-<u>v</u>alentine, **w**-<u>w</u>agon,

y-<u>y</u>ard, **z**-<u>z</u>ebra, **ck**-<u>k</u>ey

Blend Phonics Fluency Drill 1 (Unit 1)

-a- b d f g h j l m n qu p r s t v w y z ck

mat	jam	rat	map	man
ham	Nat	pad	mad	bad
fan	bag	wag	rag	sad
hag	fat	pat	tap	pan
nap	lap	Sam	lass	dad
rap	tan	Pam	gas	Ann
bat	tag	hat	nap	at
lap	Nat	pass	am	zag
mad	tan	bad	yak	bat
mass	pan	gas	rat	bag
jazz	pat	wax	Ann	pad
pat	rag	fat	tax	Pam
tag	jam	sad	sap	dad
had	an	dad	ran	van
wag	cap	tag	nap	fan
lad	rap	can	tan	cat
pass	lass	cab	Ann	pad
lap	bad	quack	fat	pat

Blend Phonics Fluency Drill 2 (Unit 2)

-i-

miss	fit	did	Jim	Jill
Sis	nip	fib	dig	bib
bit	him	sit	hip	hit
sin	sip	Bill	fig	win
rip	Tim	bin	hill	pin
will	mill	zip	dip	wig
tip	lid	big	pig	lip
fill	kill	sip	dip	jig
sit	pig	hit	nip	fig
lip	fit	dig	bill	Jim
lid	tin	pit	sin	Sis
rip	pill	did	in	hip
wig	fill	Jill	tip	bin
mix	rib	Tim	six	will
zip	fig	big	sip	lip
sip	Bill	bib	win	bit
Tim	quick	hid	kiss	vim
lid	him	nip	fib	Sis

Blend Phonics Fluency Drill 3 (Units 1, 2)

-a- -i-

bat	bit	bib	did	dad
hat	hit	hid	fat	lit
gas	hill	fill	in	an
Ann	Sam	bag	big	dip
dig	tip	tap	hip	lip
lap	ham	him	pad	pat
pit	pal	cat	sat	mad
mat	mitt	lass	mass	pass
lass	it	at	is	if
mix	Max	rig	rag	tag
jam	rat	van	vim	six
cab	zip	zap	fin	fan
fix	Tim	tam	rip	rap
nap	nip	rag	sag	wag
wig	sap	sip	map	yak
quick	quack	zig	zap	zag
Jim	jam	rig	pin	rip
mill	fill	fell	tip	sip

Blend Phonics Fluency Drill 4 (Unit 3)

-o-

Bob	log	top	hop	bog
fog	fox	box	hot	not
nod	sod	sob	pod	got
pot	rob	cob	cot	mob
rod	rot	lock	bob	pop
job	gob	doll	dot	lot
tot	on	mom	off	Don
mop	sop	moss	boss	toss
bog	hod	got	mob	pop
lop	rot	tog	bog	dog
cog	fog	bot	mob	sod
loss	pod	got	Don	Tom
boss	pop	nod	lot	mop
tot	moss	on	job	bog
nob	rob	doll	on	God
off	fox	top	box	got
lock	Bob	job	jot	lot
sod	cod	mop	pod	doll

Blend Phonics Fluency Drill 5 – (Units 1 to 3)

-a- -i- -o-

Bob	bib	bob	dot	tot
gob	got	big	bog	bag
fog	fig	hog	hag	hot
hit	hid	hat	hod	had
Nat	pod	pad	pit	pot
pat	cob	cab	nod	not
nit	sob	cot	cat	rob
rib	rod	rot	rat	mob
pop	top	tap	tip	tax
job	jab	jib	doll	dill
fill	hill	kill	lot	lit
on	an	in	log	lag
off	Don	box	fox	fix
fax	mop	map	sop	sap
sip	wag	wig	mass	miss
moss	boss	toss	loss	quick
quack	wig	top	tip	top
quick	wit	pill	till	fill

Blend Phonics Fluency Drill 6 (Unit 4)

-u-

dug	rub	bun	duck	jug
sun	bug	fun	mug	cup
rug	sum	bud	but	fuss
mud	tub	hut	bus	gum
gun	muff	muss	tug	hug
lug	nut	rut	cub	gull
pup	cuff	hum	run	cut
up	us	buzz	Gus	nut
hut	muss	cut	bus	up
us	fun	hum	run	lug
hug	cut	fun	hum	muss
mug	sum	tub	but	bud
duff	lug	cuff	mud	gun
sun	mud	muff	tug	gull
jug	dug	rub	hum	hug
dud	tug	hum	cup	us
cub	run	rum	bud	dub
fuss	muss	pup	nut	bum

Blend Phonics Fluency Drill 7 – (Units 1 to 4)

-a-　-i-　-o-　-u-

but	bat	bit	kit	kid
hut	hat	hot	hit	dug
dig	dog	bug	big	bag
bog	hug	hog	rub	rob
rod	rib	van	ban	bin
bun	duck	jug	jig	jag
sun	sin	fun	fan	fin
fix	ax	box	fox	mug
wag	wig	rug	rag	rig
sum	lass	bud	bad	bid
fuss	buzz	mud	mad	tub
tab	bus	kiss	gun	tug
tag	cup	cap	cop	nut
not	up	hill	fill	pill
till	will	gal	got	pat
pit	him	ham	run	ran
cub	cob	cab	cut	cat
wax	mix	log	quick	quack

Blend Phonics Fluency Drill 8 (Unit 5)

-e-

bell	dell	tell	fell	beg
peg	Ted	bet	let	led
fed	jet	get	pet	bed
pen	dell	red	den	hen
less	set	vet	wet	web
wed	met	net	sell	well
mess	men	ten	keg	leg
vex	meg	yes	beg	Deb
let	bet	Ted	men	fell
well	led	den	Ned	fed
sell	leg	vet	Ben	egg
yell	dell	Ed	hen	well
set	sell	peg	get	less
beg	less	led	net	den
tell	den	mess	Ben	hen
bet	men	ten	keg	wet
wed	met	get	fell	leg
less	mess	Les	vex	bed

Blend Phonics Fluency Drill 9 – (Units 1 to 5)

-a- -i- -o- -u- -e-

get	got	net	nut	not
rot	rut	rat	rod	rid
red	set	sit	sat	beg
bag	bog	bug	big	box
hen	ham	him	peg	pig
bet	bit	bat	but	bed
bid	bud	bad	let	fed
fad	fit	jet	pet	pat
wax	pen	pin	pan	web
wed	wet	doll	bill	bell
tell	hill	fell	fill	full
fox	fix	well	will	pull
den	less	loss	kiss	men
man	mom	sell	less	mass
miss	pass	yes	mop	map
mat	met	ten	tin	tan
tax	keg	buzz	kid	kit
cup	cop	cap	quack	quick

Blend Phonics Fluency Drills

Step 2

Final and Beginning Consonant Blends

and Consonant Digraphs

Drills 10 – 17

Units 6 – 15

Decodable Stories 6 - 21

Phonvisual Chart Picture-Sound Correspondences

th-<u>th</u>ree, **th**-<u>th</u>is, **ch/tch**-<u>ch</u>erry, **wh**-<u>wh</u>eel, **w**-<u>w</u>agon

ng-swi<u>ng</u>, **n**(k)-swi<u>ng</u> (ta<u>nk</u>)

Blend Phonics Fluency Drill 10 (Unit 6)
ft lk lp lt mp nd nt sk st xt ck

mend	pump	pomp	bent	hint
bend	hand	band	jump	pant
duck	dock	belt	felt	just
jest	quest	Jack	bump	lamp
lump	dump	damp	hump	camp
kick	lock	lack	lick	luck
back	desk	disk	sent	send
sand	wind	neck	fast	fist
pick	lift	loft	list	last
lost	lest	lend	land	lent
rust	rest	quack	quick	fond
fend	fund	lint	lent	tent
tint	rock	rack	melt	sick
sack	sock	gift	next	must
mast	mist	went	test	tack
tick	tock	tuck	tilt	milk
silk	sulk	gulp	end	ask
best	its	past	gust	help

Blend Phonics Fluency Drill 11 (Units 7 to 10)
Consonant Digraphs: sh, th/th, ch/tch, wh

cash	hush	dish	fish	shall
shed	shelf	shut	shot	shop
ship	wish	than	then	them
this	that	thus	bath	thick
think	thank	thump	thin	thud
with	chat	chill	witch	chin
chum	much	such	rich	match
notch	latch	fetch	hatch	chick
chop	chip	catch	patch	pitch
ditch	want	watch	was	water
wasp	wash	what	which	whisk
whack	whiff	whip	whet	whiz
when	whim	chap	chin	shed
shell	then	thud	when	what
shed	thump	bath	much	hutch
lunch	chuck	what	water	whiff
fish	ship	shop	shot	shun
wish	whish	them	fetch	cash

Blend Phonics Fluency Drill 12 (Units 11, 12)
Endings -ng, -nk

bang	ding	dong	wing	king
hung	hang	thing	thong	rang
rung	ring	sing	sung	sang
song	snug	gong	gang	long
lung	bank	bunk	link	lank
chunk	chink	mink	monk	wink
tank	thank	think	honk	kink
dunk	dank	pink	punk	rink
rank	sank	sunk	sink	ink
bang	monk	sing	long	bank
thing	thank	long	gong	rink
gang	chunk	bunk	wing	wink
song	snug	thank	bunk	sung
ding	lung	link	think	wink
honk	hunk	dank	sang	snug
snag	bang	king	wing	wink
snug	dank	bank	link	kink
lank	dink	chink	gong	gang

Blend Phonics Fluency Drill 13 (Unit 13, 15)
Initial Single Letter Consonant to Cons. Blends

rat-brat	rub-scrub	rip-grip
ring-bring	rink-drink	rag-brag
rust-crust	rip-strip	rim-brim
rip-trip	rug-drug	ramp-cramp
rust-trust	rap-strap	ring-string
rash-crash	rush-brush	rug-shrug
lump-plump	tub-stub	lap-flap
lip-clip	pan-span	lock-block
lend-blend	lack-slack	lint-splint
lap-clap	pit-spit	lip-slip
link-blink	lash-splash	lock-flock
pick-spick	wept-swept	lash-flash
pill-spill	lip-flip	lick-slick
till-still	sill-spill	lit-split

Blend Phonics Fluency Drill 14 (Unit 13)
Initial Consonant Blends: Part 1

blank	drink	chink	flog	flag
plan	plant	flung	fling	spunk
spank	flit	flat	fled	smug
smog	block	black	blast	blink
blank	blend	bland	bled	flock
flack	smell	flag	flog	smash
smelt	blush	spit	spat	spot
splat	split	bliss	stuck	stock
stick	stack	stamp	stump	stand
flop	flip	flap	stop	step
club	slap	slip	slop	clap
clip	clop	still	plod	plot
plat	glad	gland	slam	slim
slum	slosh	slash	stem	click
clack	clock	cluck	clinch	glass
gloss	cliff	scat	scalp	sled
slid	slot	slat	slit	slab
stab	stub	clink	clank	clunk

Blend Phonics Fluency Drill 15 (Unit 13)
Initial Consonant Blends: Part 2

snip	snap	skin	snob	snub
skip	skid	clench	snug	snag
sang	sung	stiff	stuff	staff
cling	clang	clung	skill	skull
skiff	scuff	scoff	swell	swill
swift	snuff	sniff	scum	scam
scan	spin	span	spun	flesh
flash	flush	sketch	flip	flap
flag	flop	switch	spell	spill
swing	swung	swim	swam	fling
flung	smack	smock	swept	swap
swag	swig	clock	cliff	plod
club	glad	plan	stuck	stack
blend	flock	smelt	clap	clinch
spot	stop	stack	glass	plod
club	clap	bliss	spill	flog
flag	stuck	blush	spit	scat
spin	scam	swap	flip	flop

Blend Phonics Fluency Drill 16 (Unit 14)
Initial Consonant Blends: Part 3

brag	drug	drag	frog	drop
drip	crunch	grin	brand	fresh
prank	brass	French	Fred	Frank
frost	brim	drank	drink	drunk
bring	drum	frock	brash	brush
brunch	branch	brink	brick	grand
grant	print	prim	press	dress
grass	crab	crib	trim	tram
tromp	trump	crash	crush	crest
crack	crust	cramp	crimp	gruff
trot	trod	crisp	truck	track
trick	trunk	trend	trust	twist
grip	grasp	crop	drill	plug
pluck	plank	grad	grid	blend
bland	blond	blast	blest	bled
glad	clang	clung	cling	swung
swing	prong	string	strung	sprung
sprang	spring	stick	stamp	crunch

Blend Phonics Fluency Drill 17 (Units 15)
Simple Short-Vowel, 2-Syllable Words

bedrock	napkin	chestnut	flapjack	sunspot
handcuff	blacktop	hubcap	landmass	ashcan
sandbag	dishpan	claptrap	midland	helmet
eggnog	shipment	backstop	laptop	catfish
kidnap	hotdog	gumdrop	endless	sonnet
dogsled	bobcat	dustpan	upland	cashbox
desktop	humbug	visit	habit	basket
ticket	rabbit	pencil	vivid	robin
puppet	sudden	husband	sunset	dental
exit	within	rocket	racket	ribbon
combat	lemon	jacket	traffic	pocket
picket	lesson	Hobbit	handbag	seven
wingspan	filmstrip	magnet	tiptop	catnap
trashcan	hilltop	nutmeg	hatchet	latchet
ratchet	upon	handstand	chicken	biggest
address	bellhop	handbag	tomcat	tinsmith
lapdog	hotdog	fishpond	upset	kitchen
stocking	exit	robin	bathtub	unfit

Blend Phonics Fluency Drills

Step 3

Long Vowel VCE Words
Long Vowel Phonograms &
Short Words with Long Vowels

Drills 18 – 26

Units 16 - 18

Decodable Stories 22 - 27

Phonvisual Chart Picture-Sound Correspondences

a-e: ā-c̲a̲ke, **e-e:** ē-tr̲ee̲, **i-e:** ī-fi̲ve, **o-e:** ō: r̲o̲se, **u-e:** ū-mu̲le

Blend Phonics Fluency Drill 18 (Unit 16)
Long ā with Final Silent e: a-e (cake)

bake	cane	cape	cake	date
daze	fate	fade	gate	gaze
hate	came	haze	lake	lame
make	mane	made	mate	late
game	wake	name	pale	quake
rate	rake	pane	sake	shame
shake	same	take	tame	blame
flame	plane	stake	glade	snake
chase	safe	paste	gave	case
fake	haste	flake	save	blaze
vase	taste	waste	brave	brake
crate	crave	craze	drape	grape
grave	trade	Dave	ape	ate
Kate	blaze	trade	Jane	blade
waste	drape	tale	crate	brave
name	plane	slave	quake	chase
spade	snake	shave	wave	thane
shake	pane	daze	pane	take

Blend Phonics Fluency Drill 19 (Unit 16)

Long ī & ē with Final Silent e: i-e (five), e-e (tree)

bite	dime	dine	dike	fine
fife	dive	file	five	hide
hive	live	drive	lime	life
like	mine	these	mile	nine
pike	pine	pile	quite	kite
ride	shine	side	spike	smile
slime	here	swine	spine	ripe
time	tile	tide	wife	wine
side	pipe	size	glide	while
white	pride	prime	prize	rile
bite	bride	quite	pile	tide
glide	hive	hide	stile	like
here	bite	hike	dike	bride
Mike	pike	dive	strife	mine
bike	ripe	chime	hive	ride
side	slide	quite	glide	bride
hire	thine	mite	strike	Pete
dike	wife	swipe	smile	like

Blend Phonics Fluency Drill 20 (Unit 16)
Long ā, ē, ī Mixed Practice

bite	gave	dine	lake	fine
Pete	size	these	pride	kite
bike	here	shame	fake	swine
taste	white	brave	quite	pale
glide	ripe	flake	paste	Pete
prize	trade	Kate	Mike	Dave
prime	waste	pile	glide	crave
Jane	chase	quake	bride	stave
spike	tale	hive	ride	slave
shake	plane	prime	craze	pipe
pane	safe	shine	flame	dive
life	drape	mile	tide	name
spade	nine	snake	side	slide
mite	lame	same	spike	bike
trade	glide	shave	lime	ape
five	Pete	prime	pane	take
thine	spine	rake	rate	wife
here	these	rile	while	pike

Blend Phonics Fluency Drill 21 (Unit 16)
Long ō with Final Silent e: o-e (r<u>o</u>se)

bone	cone	cope	code	dote
dole	dome	globe	hole	home
hope	joke	lone	lode	lope
poke	pole	quote	rode	role
rope	sole	spoke	slope	smoke
note	tone	tote	stole	mope
mole	vote	woke	broke	drove
probe	those	globe	stone	Rome
coke	scope	throne	mole	doze
joke	rode	stroke	pole	woke
stove	tone	mope	froze	globe
rope	rode	shore	sore	lore
grove	store	spoke	coke	vote
grope	note	sole	froze	wore
chore	scope	rope	tore	dome
cone	cope	mope	tone	snore
more	joke	rode	grove	doze
choke	throne	smoke	robe	vote

Blend Phonics Fluency Drill 22 (Unit 16)
Long ā, ē, ī, ō with Final Silent e (Mixed Practice)

kite	care	scare	save	wide
sole	lime	sale	blame	while
ripe	rode	kite	shake	smile
tone	scope	throne	cake	poke
more	square	mole	spade	choke
glare	broke	Rome	Dave	smoke
life	bride	tame	skate	grade
rode	Pete	note	chime	male
flame	save	twine	base	make
glide	time	spine	hole	hike
late	drove	these	blaze	grape
strike	tire	cane	wire	slate
date	pave	safe	life	flame
grape	gape	slime	rake	tire
grope	grave	mine	lime	smoke
wine	slide	broke	gale	paste
poste	here	size	grape	hole
note	chime	clime	rode	dare

Blend Phonics Fluency Drill 23 (Unit 16)
Long ū with Final Silent e: u-e (mule)

cube	duke	dune	cute	tube
tune	mule	flute	prune	rule
rule	rude	plume	brute	Luke
mute	fluke	duke	use	pure
fuse	tube	cube	mule	tube
sure	brute	tube	rube	June
cure	mule	prune	cube	flute
fuse	tune	fluke	duke	tune
Luke	use	duke	tube	mute
lute	Rube	brute	mule	tube
prune	tune	use	cure	Luke
tube	muse	prune	mute	rule
cube	crude	pure	lute	mule
lube	mule	duke	fluke	use
cure	pure	fluke	cute	lure
flute	cute	June	Rube	Luke
cure	pure	rule	crude	lute
use	tube	mute	brute	cure

Blend Phonics Fluency Drill 24 (Unit 16)
Long ā, ē, ī, ō, ū with Final Silent e (Mixed)

pane	fluke	tune	waste	use
bake	cube	swine	note	paste
those	time	save	vote	tile
wife	mope	haste	fake	spine
haste	wide	haze	white	cute
lake	dune	file	made	bone
broke	game	five	brave	mule
name	home	wake	hide	pale
like	Pete	crate	hive	late
role	lime	ate	poke	mile
take	poke	shake	grape	sake
mile	snake	mine	shade	pine
rode	pride	pole	nine	take
pile	quote	quite	rode	prime
kite	tame	probe	tape	ride
blame	rope	flute	stone	stake
plane	rule	flame	hope	robe
smoke	here	brute	chose	side

Blend Phonics Fluency Drill 25 (Units 17 & 18)
Long Vowel: Phonograms & Short Words

old	bold	scold	cold	gold
fold	told	sold	mold	hold
colt	volt	molt	bolt	jolt
toll	roll	post	most	host
both	mild	child	wild	rind
wind	blind	find	grind	hind
kind	mind	be	he	no
she	go	me	so	we
I	the	old	mind	wild
kind	sold	blind	jolt	fold
hold	kind	scold	child	mild
both	told	molt	host	rind
mind	roll	toll	so	he
no	go	grind	cold	most
post	he	she	me	hold
host	be	kind	volt	I
so	child	no	go	wind
both	we	wild	child	most

Blend Phonics Fluency Drill 26 (Units 1-18)
Mixed Short and Long Vowel Review

cap	cape	past	paste	back
bake	rid	ride	go	so
me	rat	rate	gap	gape
fad	fade	was	brag	dim
dime	kit	kite	site	sit
note	not	tub	tube	rid
ride	robe	rob	snack	snake
sang	cub	cube	pet	Pete
at	ate	quake	quack	quick
hate	hat	hop	hope	back
black	ride	rid	chat	water
was	what	fish	he	shell
fix	tax	yes	kiss	lass
moss	next	gulp	tent	ship
shop	mash	bath	the	with
chat	catch	press	fog	frog
did	bib	bed	crust	brush
shake	wife	taste	plane	hot

Blend Phonics Fluency Drills

Step 4

R-Controlled Vowels

Drills 27 – 31

Units 19 - 21

Decodable Stories 28 - 31

Phonvisual Chart Picture-Sound Correspondences

ar: c<u>ar</u>, **or:** f<u>or</u>k, **er/ir/ur/or:** f<u>ur</u>

Blend Phonics Fluency Drill 27 (Unit 19)
Phonogram ar (c<u>ar</u>)

bar	dark	dart	tart	mark
hark	bark	scar	barn	darn
far	mart	star	car	farm
park	tar	chart	start	cart
hard	part	jar	spark	lark
smart	starch	stark	art	arch
march	harm	yarn	sharp	arm
charm	harmless	harvest	part	warm
march	harmful	harm	lard	bark
Mark	scarf	yarn	part	smart
are	card	tar	park	March
march	hard	chart	arm	farm
part	dart	darting	sharp	star
marsh	harsh	cart	jar	harp
harm	art	mar	yard	darn
arch	arm	ark	hark	smart
jar	Mark	star	barn	far
tar	shark	park	snarl	Carl

Blend Phonics Fluency Drill 28 (Unit 20)
Phonogram or (f<u>or</u>k)

born	horn	thorn	fork	torn
cord	cork	fort	scorn	torch
scorch	corn	horse	storm	for
pork	porch	stork	worn	north
sort	short	or	nor	before
morn	morning	Lord	stork	fort
forth	worn	fort	sort	corn
morn	or	cork	pork	torch
thorn	porch	for	cord	ford
torn	sport	north	short	pork
port	tort	sort	port	fork
form	north	forth	horn	morn
short	forth	storm	corn	torn
scorch	tort	scorn	form	horn
north	corn	form	north	porch
fork	Lord	horn	born	stork
sort	short	fork	or	for
fort	port	cork	pork	or

Blend Phonics Fluency Drill 29 (Unit 21)
Phonograms er, ir, ur, and sometimes or (f<u>ur</u>)

bird	stir	fir	birth	dirt
first	girl	sir	third	clerk
fern	her	jerk	herd	term
runner	camper	cutter	sitter	catcher
starter	chopper	swimmer	dipper	sender
drummer	spinner	helper	jumper	marker
farmer	pitcher	after	better	never
mister	under	matter	batter	bitter
sister	mister	blister	dinner	summer
winter	tender	skipper	ladder	madder
gladder	hammer	slumber	litter	miller
glummer	slimmer	winner	hurt	curb
planner	curl	fur	purr	turn
burn	doctor	factor	janitor	actor
work	worm	world	visitor	worst
word	worker	church	Bert	perch
chirp	squirm	curl	shirt	hers
thirst	fur	jerk	herd	burst

Blend Phonics Fluency Drill 30 (Units 19, 20, 21)
R-Controlled Vowels (Mixed Words)

bird	horn	bar	first	thorn
first	cork	dark	storm	girl
north	far	shirt	barn	for
third	park	burn	starch	corn
mart	short	spark	herd	porch
star	term	yarn	horn	harm
hurt	scorn	starch	thirst	cart
smart	worst	fork	Lord	sharp
church	Mark	chirp	bark	chirp
torch	port	pork	warm	farm
nor	ladder	sport	form	port
doctor	sister	her	lard	chart
charm	sort	morning	cord	fort
cork	never	herd	jerk	curl
stark	starch	start	porch	fort
perch	burst	form	ford	part
fur	fir	matter	after	fern
sir	under	winter	dirt	arch

Blend Phonics Fluency Drill 31 (Units 1 - 21)
Review of Steps 1, 2, 3, and 4

car	cord	late	brag	her
he	ship	her	nurse	fur
ate	storm	was	truck	fire
spike	paste	form	when	fir
what	size	that	latch	work
glide	crate	quote	flute	turn
drove	cold	wild	gold	burn
find	the	smart	charm	pole
black	dark	morning	world	wild
never	farmer	doctor	lack	find
lake	Mack	make	wake	tin
slam	switch	on	clock	kind
cute	cod	slope	flute	brag
up	tube	smoke	cone	tile
fin	fine	shame	lip	code
grape	dishpan	handstand	picnic	run
hilltop	duck	quick	quack	cork
quit	bug	cave	mule	grass

Blend Phonics Fluency Drills

Step 5

Vowel Digraphs & Diphthongs

Drills 32 - 47

Units 22 - 35

Decodable Stories 22 - 49

Phonvisual Chart Picture-Sound Correspondences

ay/ai: c<u>a</u>ke; **ee:** tr<u>ee</u>; **ea:** tr<u>ee</u>, b<u>e</u>d, c<u>a</u>ke; **ie:** f<u>i</u>ve, tr<u>ee</u>

y: tr<u>ee</u>, f<u>i</u>ve; **oa/oe:** r<u>o</u>se; **ow:** r<u>o</u>se, c<u>ow</u>; **ou:** c<u>ow</u>;

oy/oi: b<u>oy</u>; **oo:** m<u>oo</u>n, b<u>oo</u>k; **aw/au:** s<u>aw</u>; **al/all:** s<u>aw</u>

Blend Phonics Fluency Drill 32 (Unit 22)
Vowel Digraphs ai, ay: (ate)

ail	paid	pail	may	bail
bait	laid	lay	bay	hay
day	brain	clay	gray	fail
rail	pay	pray	grain	gain
drain	rain	ray	sail	say
jail	tail	trail	sway	maid
train	jay	gay	way	wail
mail	wait	plain	play	claim
strain	strait	pain	paint	faint
chair	tray	railway	runway	away
chain	aim	pray	strain	hair
maid	clay	quaint	drain	ray
chair	pair	bray	say	rail
sway	fair	lay	nay	mail
ray	gray	trail	mail	bay
faint	pair	paid	aim	Cain
wail	pay	saint	stray	sway
may	Kay	May	quail	sail

Blend Phonics Fluency Drill 33 (Unit 23, 24)
Long Vowel Digraphs ēe, ēa: (tr<u>ee</u>)

bee	keen	sleet	beef	free
peep	sweep	beech	freeze	peek
sweet	beet	fleet	reed	sheep
deed	green	see	meet	deep
greet	seed	need	breeze	heed
heel	seen	wee	fee	seem
weed	feet	feel	feed	jeep
sleep	peel	keep	sleeve	weep
three	beat	each	reach	read
beach	leaf	beast	leap	real
bean	leave	cream	lean	cheat
meal	cheap	least	deal	sea
dream	seat	feast	treat	team
tea	east	teach	eat	feat
peach	steal	fear	near	clean
scream	steel	steal	deer	dear
seem	seam	week	weak	leap
meet	meat	teem	team	queen

Blend Phonics Fluency Drill 34 (Unit 24)
Vowel Digraphs ĕa, eā

ĕa (bĕd)

threat	thread	tread	bread	wealth
read	weather	breath	dead	death
health	instead	deaf	sweat	treading
sweater	spread	treads	heather	head
heaven	leaven	sweats	threads	stead

eā (cāke)

steak	break	great	bear	breaker
daybreak	swear	tear	bears	wear

ĕa, eā mixed

read	tear	pears	wear	head
health	break	bears	death	wealth
sweater	daybreak	breath	weather	swearing
tread	swear	deaf	sweat	head
heather	breaker	instead	health	breaker
wear	bread	tread	weather	great
heaven	stead	leaven	thread	treading

Blend Phonics Fluency Drill 35 (Units 25)
Vowel Digraph ie: īe and iē

īe: (five)

cried	lies	tied	cries	lied
tried	dried	pie	dries	pies
spies	fried	lie	tie	ties

iē: (tree)

priest	relief	believe	brief	chief
yield	grief	field	thief	priests

Mixed īe, iē

chief	cried	pie	field	tie
tried	thief	lie	priests	cries
yield	pies	grief	dries	dried
believe	lied	ties	grief	tied
pies	brief	lied	thief	yields

Blend Phonics Fluency Drill 36 (Unit 26)

y = ī in 1-syllable words; y = ĭ (or ē) in Polysyllables

army	handy	sleepy	my	candy
hilly	thirty	ply	guppy	healthy
twenty	sly	daddy	bunny	silly
try	dolly	fifty	wealthy	sky
dusty	messy	shy	funny	penny
by	why	gummy	puppy	cry
party	rainy	dry	happy	sunny
fly	myself	pretty	foggy	Henry
copy	sloppy	sixty	flimsy	pry
sandy	spy	fishy	witty	by
windy	puppy	try	penny	messy
dandy	my	sadly	fly	empty
dizzy	jelly	Jimmy	silly	thirty
sky	daddy	Billy	gladly	grumpy
sandy	shy	sadly	madly	sky
shy	fly	army	candy	my
my	myself	sixty	fishy	funny
sloppy	by	hungry	starry	sky

Blend Phonics Fluency Drill 37 (Unit 27)

Long ō Vowel Digraphs oa, oe (r<u>o</u>se)

boat	load	roast	Joe	boast
loaf	soap	toe	coat	road
toes	coach	soapy	foe	woe
coast	soak	goes	goat	toad
hoe	float	throat	hoed	board
coal	oak	cloak	foam	loam
goad	toast	bloat	oat	goes
whoa	loan	oats	hoe	Joe
Moe	goal	goals	goad	load
goat	foe	doe	woe	roam
toe	soak	boast	boat	boats
hoe	roast	loaf	groan	toes
oak	roam	Joe	toads	coach
oats	boast	toe	toes	loads
roads	goads	boat	toads	boat
foam	toes	hoes	soak	groan
roast	roasts	hoe	Joe	moat
soak	oats	doe	toe	toad

Blend Phonics Fluency Drill 38 (Unit 28)

Digraph ow; Diphthong ow

Digraph ōw: (r<u>o</u>se)

bow	slow	window	bowl	blow
throw	yellow	crow	show	glow
shown	grow	snow	grown	fellow
growth	follow	flow	hollow	low
pillow	shadow	shown	own	row

Diphthong ow: (c<u>ow</u>)

frown	flower	gown	growl	cow
howl	crowd	power	how	clown
powder	crown	drown	town	down
brown	now	sow	howls	prowl

Mixed ow Practice

slow	frown	crow	flower	sow
brown	crown	low	blow	cow
pillow	flow	powder	hollow	clown
shadow	crowd	glow	drown	grow
show	own	how	crown	blows

Blend Phonics Fluency Drill 39 (Units 28, 29)

Diphthongs ou, ow: (c<u>ow</u>)

out	found	flour	south	town
count	scout	cow	pound	cloud
pouch	loud	down	ground	our
mouth	howl	pout	sound	sour
drown	crouch	fowl	gown	mouth
owl	grouch	gown	round	out
crown	clown	drown	clown	spout
stout	round	trout	prowl	stout
hound	scout	count	ouch	south
flower	powder	proud	scout	how
town	cloud	mouth	brown	out
proud	spout	growl	pouch	pout
sprout	down	crown	wound	ground
fowl	flour	foul	drown	hound
pound	flower	bow	plow	stout
trout	flout	sour	bow	fowl
growl	brow	hound	sound	grouch
mouth	pouch	couch	out	clout

Blend Phonics Fluency Drill 40 (Unit 30)
Diphthongs oy, oi: (b<u>oy</u>)

toys	boil	coy	coin	point
point	oyster	foist	joy	toil
oil	Troy	broil	foil	join
spoil	coin	spoil	Roy	boy
boys	coy	soil	boil	cloy
moist	oil	Roy	soil	toil
cloy	loin	toil	point	joys
coil	boil	soy	joy	join
joins	join	soil	join	broil
joy	coil	toil	soil	moist
toil	loin	foil	joint	joints
oil	boy	point	oink	hoist
foist	hoist	point	Troy	Roy
coy	coin	coins	coils	coil
hoist	Roy	boil	toil	toy
toys	point	coin	join	joys
spoil	toil	Troy	boy	Loy
loin	coin	joy	boil	foil

Blend Phonics Fluency Drill 41 (Unit 22-30)

-y & Vowel Digraphs & Diphthongs (Mixed Practice)

loin	coin	joy	boil	foil
toys	town	army	boat	read
cow	great	day	paid	sheep
crown	daddy	by	pie	head
bread	hay	goat	Joe	soak
why	by	brown	break	bears
crow	crowd	power	flour	shy
messy	daddy	loin	weather	sadly
shy	toast	deer	dear	sea
see	rainy	oil	crow	own
pillow	show	steak	funny	bunny
dry	real	teach	sandy	mail
cream	fear	flower	shown	coin
Roy	cry	cried	field	happy
thief	hoe	toe	dead	pray
paid	petty	fly	glow	grow
rainbow	flow	Roy	yield	toad
steal	steel	copy	fishy	my

Blend Phonics Fluency Drill 42 (Unit 31)

Long o͞o: (mo͞on)

boot	moon	stoop	foolish	booth
roof	spoon	smooth	bloom	loose
spool	coo	room	shoot	spoon
noonday	cool	proof	too	boost
toothbrush	mood	tool	scooter	droop
gloom	tooth	papoose	food	noon
troop	tooting	groom	soon	tool
coolness	goose	roost	zoo	doom
smoother	stool	cooler	scoop	pool
loop	broom	root	roomy	hoot
groove	choose	soothe	boom	boot
cool	moon	coo	moo	loose
proof	bloom	zoo	smooth	scoop
tooth	loose	fool	pool	spoon
smooth	spooky	scooter	choose	doom
school	broom	room	roomy	cool
room	broom	groom	smooth	food
teaspoon	croon	fool	zoom	tool

Blend Phonics Fluency Drill 43 (Unit 32)
Short Sound of o͝o: (b<u>oo</u>k)

book	good	hood	shook	foot
booklet	look	wool	cook	soot
footstep	looking	wood	crook	hook
goodness	wooden	brook	hoof	took
woolen	cooker	hook	stood	book
shook	book	nook	foot	look
fishhook	took	shook	footer	stood
woodpile	look	hook	foot	book
woodshed	brook	took	soot	wood
plywood	wooden	hood	rook	hook
book	shook	brook	hood	soot
cook	hood	sooty	cookie	hoof
stood	cookout	hook	took	crook
look	unhook	nook	wood	brook
fishhook	foot	rook	woof	wool
plywood	rook	brook	foot	book
good	rookie	hook	look	soot
foot	look	soot	brook	hook

Blend Phonics Fluency Drill 44 (Unit 31, 32)

Long o͞o: (m<u>oo</u>n), Short ŏŏ: (b<u>oo</u>k) (Mixed Practice)

foot	moon	good	stoop	loose
shook	room	spoon	book	foot
troop	gloom	look	foot	hood
pool	spoon	rook	look	rookie
good	wood	troop	choose	moo
stood	look	pool	cooker	good
tooth	smooth	look	school	roost
zoo	shook	hook	foot	book
soot	moon	spooky	scooter	roomy
cool	footstep	hoof	gloom	proof
bloom	took	wood	tooth	school
groove	goose	wool	smooth	bloom
loose	croon	brook	hood	nook
mood	cook	foot	hoof	cool
noon	book	took	room	shoot
shoo	smooth	brook	rook	tool
cooker	shook	bloom	loose	noon
roof	look	book	boom	soon

Vowel Digraphs aw, au & a(ll): (s<u>aw</u>)

crawl	bald	hawk	call	saw
salt	clause	crawling	shawl	halt
draw	mall	drawn	also	dawn
fall	lawn	law	almost	malt
tall	thaw	haul	yaw	yawn
fault	fawn	faun	cause	false
all	pause	ball	paw	jaw
already	saw	false	draw	wall
small	dawn	stall	hawk	gall
gawk	always	chalk	launch	fault
thaw	crawl	drawl	salt	sprawl
cause	haul	yawn	drawn	also
yawn	all	jaw	paw	pawn
ball	dawn	call	calm	drawn
bald	saw	hawk	fall	paws
balls	pause	lawns	salts	shawl
crawl	malts	launch	small	draws
bald	tall	thaws	shawls	yaw

Blend Phonics Fluency Drill 46 (Units 35)

Digraphs ew, ue: (m<u>u</u>le)

blew	flew	news	flue	brew
threw	pew	glue	chew	dew
stew	true	crew	few	due
drew	mew	blue	hue	grew
new	clue	Sue	brew	chew
slew	curfew	mildew	few	screw
fewer	blues	chews	pursue	clue
rescue	statue	tissue	sue	cue
value	blew	new	news	glues
pew	flue	pews	blew	blue
hue	chew	slew	due	dues
few	fewer	statue	dew	threw
brew	few	hue	blue	chews
fewer	hew	flew	true	blue
blues	drew	hue	hues	Sue
curfew	values	threw	clue	mew
whew	blew	brews	Sue's	cues
blues	clues	flew	drew	Lew

aw, au & a(ll) and ew, ue (Mixed Practice)

crawl	blew	call	flue	stew
salt	also	crew	blue	stall
few	always	blues	dawn	hawk
call	chew	slew	yawn	jaw
flew	chalk	malt	blew	blues
saw	pew	faun	fawn	wall
bald	fewer	statute	paw	gall
threw	ball	true	shawl	false
gawk	chew	hawk	mall	brew
few	paw	fault	value	whew
lawn	sprawl	Sue	few	yawn
clause	crawl	halt	saw	shawl
malt	fewer	false	yaw	thaw
always	tissue	chews	clue	salt
law	gall	new	brew	true
saw	bald	crawl	chew	hew
sue	curfew	rescue	news	brew
slew	thaw	fawn	pew	yaw

Blend Phonics Fluency Drills

Step 6

Irregular Spelling Patterns

Drills 48 - 61

Units 36 - 47

Decodable Stories 36 - 62

Phonvisual Chart Picture-Sound Correspondences

Initial unaccented a = /ŭ/ = /ə/ (d<u>u</u>ck)   c = /s/ (<u>s</u>aw) with e, i, & y
g = /j/ (jar)   u = Short o͞o (bo͞ok),
Silent k, w, t, b, l, and gh   ph & gh = /f/ (<u>f</u>an)
le = l (<u>l</u>eaf)   tion/sion = sh (<u>sh</u>ip)
ed = ĕd, t, d (b<u>ed</u>, <u>t</u>op, <u>d</u>uck)

Blend Phonics Fluency Drill 48 (Units 36)
Unaccented a at beginning of words: ŭ (du̲ck)

a	ajar	around	asleep	about
alike	arouse	astir	adrift	ahead
apart	awake	amuse	aside	awhile
alone	ahead	amiss	a	awake
aloud	arrears	arrange	appoint	a
account	astound	amount	ado	above
ahead	alive	among	adult	about
away	awhile	amuse	afraid	agree
agreed	against	a	aside	aloud
amiss	ahead	apart	asleep	around
arouse	amiss	awake	aloud	ajar
astir	a	apart	arrange	amount
away	agree	alive	amiss	awake
award	alas	agree	astound	ahead
about	arrange	aloud	above	aloof
alight	align	adult	adjust	abut
among	also	a	amuse	among
awake	about	align	alight	alone

Blend Phonics Fluency Drill 49 (Units 32 & 37)
Short sound of o͝o spelled oo, u, & -ould

careful	book	full	cook	fullback
cooker	put	pull	look	push
soot	dull	wool	bull	wood
bush	could	fulfill	took	pulley
hood	bully	good	butcher	booklet
bulletin	could	book	should	woof
would	rook	pull	crook	bush
shook	took	put	wood	woof
pulley	crook	cookie	brook	put
bull	wool	sooty	hook	butcher
good	bush	pull	push	good
stood	soot	foot	bully	could
pull	would	push	should	soot
took	hook	book	books	bulls
hoofs	brooks	dull	pulley	woods
cookies	cook	put	puts	crooks
shook	would	good	bullies	could
books	look	book	push	should

Blend Phonics Fluency Drill 50 (Unit 38)

Soft c (before e, i, & y); /sh/ in <u>su</u>gar & spe<u>ci</u>al

cent	brace	mice	rice	cell
ocean	chance	space	cease	decide
special	niece	nice	slice	fence
center	dance	pace	spice	civil
dunce	place	since	cinder	face
peace	piece	cider	twice	special
cyclone	fleece	trace	circus	fence
prance	price	prince	princess	thence
cinch	France	precious	choice	hence
voice	acid	ice	pencil	cistern
musician	lace	ace	mince	race
cell	rice	mice	twice	lace
grace	face	trace	price	city
dance	pace	circus	nice	slices
fence	hence	cell	cease	brace
mace	trace	space	cent	special
voices	princess	prince	hence	ocean
fleece	cider	peace	piece	face

Blend Phonics Fluency Drill 51 (Unit 39)

Soft g in dge and sometimes before e, i, or y

age	page	badge	budge	bridge
ridge	plunge	dodge	lodge	ledge
smudge	change	rage	edge	wedge
cage	range	fudge	ginger	engage
sage	stage	hedge	giraffe	fringe
gist	huge	wage	nudge	giblet
barge	large	urge	pledge	gyp
gypsy	lunge	hinge	judge	gem
George	magic	stages	gym	largest
germ	ages	pages	huge	fringe
largest	urge	bridge	changes	wages
judges	ginger	range	stages	stages
giraffes	sage	badges	lodging	edger
lodge	hedge	George	gypsies	lunges
badges	nudge	range	Marge	Madge
gist	gypsy	gypsies	gems	edge
smudge	huge	smudge	lunge	fudge
giants	rage	gymnast	hedge	gist

Blend Phonics Fluency Drill 52 (Unit 40)

Silent gh and gh like /f/ in lau<u>gh</u>
Long ī with silent gh: igh (f<u>i</u>ve)

bright	high	blight	tight	might
slight	thigh	fight	flight	fighter
night	right	plight	sigh	light
moonlight	brighter	sunlight	lighter	fright

au & ou /aw/ of (s<u>aw</u>) with silent gh

taught	caught	daughter	slaughter
thought	haughty	naughty	thoughts

gh - /f/ (<u>f</u>an)

rough	tough	laugh	laughter
laughing	enough	cough	trough

Mixed Spelling Patterns

bright	rough	laugh	plight	sigh
sign	thought	blight	fight	laugh
laughing	enough	light	daughter	night
might	slight	haughty	tight	sign

Blend Phonics Fluency Drill 53 (Unit 41)
Silent k, w, t, b, l and h.

knee	kneel	knelt	knight	knife
knit	knot	known	know	knock
wrist	wring	wrap	wreck	wrote
wreath	wren	wrench	write	wretch
wrong	answer	sword	glisten	hasten
chasten	listen	often	soften	comb
numb	lamb	limb	thumb	climb
dumb	crumb	plumbing	doubt	debt
half	walk	calf	knight	comb
knife	know	listen	wren	wrong
soften	ghost	answer	climb	kneel
soften	wrench	hasten	know	sword
doubt	wrens	writes	listen	wrap
often	knife	know	glisten	hasten
comb	numb	honest	wretch	knit
honest	kneel	knee	lamb	thumb
hour	doubt	doubter	climber	knives
swords	known	knights	wrecks	lambs

Blend Phonics Fluency Drill 54 (Unit 42)
Letter s with the sound of z (z̲ebra)

choose	noise	please	those	chose
nose	rose	wise	cheese	pause
rise	as	ease	pose	tease
has	because	praise	these	is
his	games	tunes	hose	fuse
busy	visit	flies	use	raise
shoes	easy	confuse	eyes	mows
flows	boxes	wishes	dishes	ages
teaches	fixes	buses	nurses	judges
churches	witches	bosses	kisses	rise
nose	hose	shoes	eyes	wise
please	choose	has	as	raise
pause	those	is	games	his
pose	dishes	fixes	has	ease
nurses	cheese	chose	tease	fuse
mows	busy	visit	dishes	judges
ages	has	tunes	raise	rise
fuse	visit	churches	pause	pose

Blend Phonics Fluency Drill 55 (Unit 43)
ph like /f/ & gh as in rough (fan)

elephant	prophet	phonograph	telegraph	earphone
phrase	laugh	photo	phone	roughly
alphabet	Phil	pamphlet	orphan	phonogram
tough	alphabet	laughter	telephone	cough
phone	laughter	hyphen	Philip	Ralph
pharmacy	photon	autograph	elephant	triumph
phone	tough	alphabet	phone	phrase
laugh	rough	prophet	pamphlet	nephew
hyphen	Phil	Ralph	enough	tough
phrase	Philip	alphabet	pharmacy	phonogram
nephew	phone	phonics	laughter	laugh
hyphen	alphabet	trough	alphabet	nephew
orphan	phone	pamphlet	telegraph	Ralph
elephant	phrase	enough	photo	phone
cough	orphan	autograph	phone	rough
photo	alphabet	photograph	enough	laugh
Ralph	phase	phrase	elephant	prophet
nephew	hyphen	telegraph	pharmacy	tough

Blend Phonics Fluency Drill 56 (Unit 44)
Final le (leaf), tion, sion (ship)

battle	handle	bottle	bundle	puzzle
scramble	buckle	little	sprinkle	pickle
circle	struggle	middle	tickle	wiggle
attention	sample	scribble	partition	action
portion	addition	station	nation	little
affection	invitation	foundation	mission	bottle
expression	education	mention	station	battle
section	cattle	rifle	fiction	handle
nation	battle	baffle	tackle	fiddle
education	trickle	mission	station	cattle
ration	Bible	candle	occasion	able
permission	question	election	bottle	table
mansion	uncle	expression	patient	apple
mention	saddle	education	addiction	jungle
pension	fiction	puzzles	battle	station
question	fraction	jungle	jingle	ruffle
faction	fiddle	television	humble	single
addition	tickle	fiction	angle	needle

Blend Phonics Fluency Drill 57 (Unit 45)
Past Tense Ending ed: (ĕd, d, t)

added	ended	painted	waited	acted
folded	planted	counted	landed	printed
crowded	lighted	rested	graded	seated
sifted	petted	tested	needed	twisted
roasted	mended	aimed	changed	saved
stayed	burned	filled	rained	turned
called	named	rolled	sailed	peeled
pinned	kneeled	claimed	loaned	roared
climbed	wheeled	scattered	cleaned	canned
plowed	baked	backed	picked	packed
looked	locked	wished	boxed	hoped
hopped	packed	camped	jumped	pitched
hitched	liked	stopped	kissed	coaxed
guessed	dropped	checked	shipped	talked
scraped	dashed	milked	draped	worked
clapped	wrecked	wrapped	stamped	dressed
knocked	stalled	happened	worked	jumped

Blend Phonics Fluency Drill 58 (Unit 45+)
Adding Endings ing, y, ier, iest, ily

rob	robbing	slip	slipping	slipped
hop	hopping	bad	berry	berries
happy	happily	dip	dipping	stunning
tan	tanning	fade	fading	go
going	press	sag	sagging	pressing
care	caring	dizzy	dizzier	dizziest
Bob	Bobby	sleep	sleepy	sleepier
crazy	crazily	crazier	craziest	fog
foggy	mess	messy	messier	hurry
cherry	cherries	nap	napping	hug
hugging	beg	tap	begging	tapping
candy	candies	nut	nutty	nuttier
nuttiest	baby	babies	setting	napping
skipping	silly	silliest	bunny	bunnies
chilly	chillier	thirsty	thirstier	hardly
story	stories	army	armies	top
topping	marry	fishy	marrying	daddy
messiest	trimming	pup	puppy	puppies

Blend Phonics Fluency Drill 59 (Unit 46)
Long Vowels in Open Syllables

baker	racer	oval	shady	fever
lady	cedar	grocer	paper	hero
oral	caper	legal	final	open
taper	regal	tulip	favor	before
bony	Lucy	savor	tidy	pony
vapor	limy	holy	wafer	slimy
over	maker	viper	clover	taker
biter	donor	pupil	nasal	solar
fatal	polar	mural	natal	libel
sober	rural	label	cider	local
tyro	halo	spider	focal	tyrant
sago	tiger	vocal	pacer	vital
total	giant	poem	pliant	dial
trial	vial	duel	fuel	cruel
gruel	brier	ruin	friar	tidy
Lucy	Macy	dial	trial	hero
zero	super	cradle	ladle	legal
bony	pupil	student	taker	halo

Blend Phonics Fluency Drill 60 (Unit 47)
37 Dolch List Service Words & 3 /zh/ Words

do	to	today	together	two
who	into	come	done	does
some	one	once	of	from
again	said	could	would	any
many	only	are	carry	eight
have	give	their	they	very
where	were	every	been	buy
don't	your	measure	pleasure	two
treasure	could	once	to	do
some	together	does	said	many
of	from	are	give	today
together	into	who	do	would
would	every	pleasure	very	buy
buy	have	been	any	where
don't	measure	carry	two	into
been	two	would	their	are
treasure	come	done	once	today
again	many	only	said	of

Blend Phonics Fluency Drill 61
Three- and Four-Syllable Words

liberty	independence	blueberries	democracy
Thanksgiving	Elizabeth	secretary	February
transportation	dictionary	asparagus	understand
restaurant	president	Mississippi	afternoon
musician	unhappiness	American	holiday
newspaper	gorilla	suddenly	miserable
awkwardly	surprising	invitation	vanilla
conversation	merchandise	perfection	decision
beginning	favorite	December	earnestly
January	surrounded	lecturer	accident
amazing	committee	permanent	tomorrow
attractive	peevishly	together	wonderful
entertain	fashionable	impossible	threatening
vinegar	Cinderella	exciting	mysterious
refreshments	thunderstorm	practical	banana
selfishly	exchanging	impatience	emperor
correction	Valentine	medicine	banister
butterfly	passengers	jealously	family
exclaiming	Washington	quizzical	emergency
innocent	difficulty	ordinary	underneath

Suggested Oral Reading Speeds

Rapid word processing (identification) speeds are an accurate indicator of decoding automaticity. The faster a student can decode words while maintaining accuracy, the higher the degree of automaticity. Good comprehension depends on decoding automaticity: higher automaticity makes possible higher comprehension. An automatic response is one that requires little or no conscious thought or effort.

In the rush for higher word processing speeds, it is very important not to skip any essential sub-skill. Whole-word readers sometimes appear to initially read faster than phonics-readers; but in the long run, their faulty word processing strategies lead to lower automaticity, and therefore, lower comprehension.

Word processing skills (speed and accuracy) can be accurately measured by timing student's oral reading on the words in Donald L. Potter's *Blend Phonics Timed Fluency Drills*. The speeds recommended by the original *Victory Drill Book* (1970) reflect years of highly successful experience teaching similar exercises to children of every age. They are one-minute timings.

Minimum Speed for Page Mastery

Grade	Speed
Pre-Kindergarten	20 words per minute
Kindergarten	30 words per minute
First Grade	40 words per minute
Second Grade	55 words per minute
Third Grade	70 words per minute
Fourth Grade	85 words per minute
Fifth Grade	100 words per minute
Sixth Grade	115 words per minute
Seventh Grade	130 words per minute
Eight Grade	130 words per minute

Once the students have mastered the *Timed Drills*, they should start every year with a rapid review of all the *Drills*. Each student's speed should be measured to assure that they are able to read the words at the calibrated speed for their grade level. This review is very valuable for all students, regardless of their reading ability.

The timings are also diagnostic in that students new to the school will be automatically screened as to their reading ability. Every effort should be made to help slower students reach the minimum calibrated speed for their grade level. Remember that students of all ages and ability levels can benefit from phonics instruction.

The timings are so easy that parents and peers can do them with a minimum of training. Any one-minute timer will work. Simply move a pointer over the words from left to right as the student reads the words, pausing if a student makes an error. Every self-correction is a move forward toward strengthening left-brain decoding and discouraging whole-word guessing. Keep a record of the students' timings and note the increases. Move to the next Drill once the students have attained the calibrated speed for their grade level. Speeds are suggestions based on wide experience, but they should be adjusted to individual student ability. Sometimes it is necessary to reduce the speed the first time through for struggling students.

Foundation for Phonics

26 Letters (minus 3 superfluous letters, *c, q, x*) for 44 Sounds

25 Consonant Sounds

<u>18 Consonant Pairs</u>

<u>Voiced</u>   <u>Unvoiced</u>

1.	/b/	*bib*		2.	/p/	*pup*
3.	/d/	*dad*		4.	/t/	*toot*
5.	/g/	*gag*		6.	/k/	*kick*
7.	/z/	*zig-zag*		8.	/s/	*Sis*
9.	/v/	*valve*		10.	/f/	*fluff*
11.	/th/	*then*		12.	/th/	*thistle*
13.	/w/	*wayward*		14.	/hw/	*whistle*
15.	/j/	*jam*		16.	/ch/	*chick*
17.	/zh/	*treasure*		18.	/sh/	*trash*

<u>6 Consonants called Semivowels:</u>

19. /l/   *lull*
20. /m/   *mom*
21. /n/   *nun*
22. /r/   *run*
23. /y/   *yo-yo*
24. /ng/ *singing*

<u>1 more consonant:</u>

25. /h/   *his*

We have used 19 letters to write 25 consonants: b, c, d, f, g, h, j, k, l, m, n, p, r, s, t, v, w, y, and z. Two more are superfluous letters representing consonant combinations: q and x. We have used 21 of the 26 letters to write 25 consonant sounds. $26 - 19 = 5$

This leaves us exactly 5 letters – a, e, i, o, u – to deal with 19 vowel sounds.

The 19 Vowel Sounds

5 So-called short vowels:
26. /ă/ *bag*
27. /ĕ/ *beg*
28. /ĭ/ *big*
29. /ŏ/ *bog*
30. /ŭ/ *bug*

5 So-called long vowels:
31. /ā/ *mate*   (*aim, may*)
32. /ē/ *mete*   (*see, sea*)
33. /ī/ *mite*   (*my, light*)
34. /ō/ *mote*   (*boat, toe, tow*)
35. /ū/ *mute*   (*blue, blew*)

3 diphthongs:
36. /au/   *Paul, crawl*
37. /ou/   *spouse, cow*
38. /oi/   *noise, boy*

2 sounds for oo, short and long:
39. /o͝o/   *push, whoosh*
40. /o͞o/   *Rube, moon*

1 sound of *a* in *ma*:
41. /ä/ *pa, ma; bar, car*

2 r sounds:
42. /air/ *fair, heir, dare, swear*
43. /ûr/ *girl, prefer, fur, doctor*

All purpose muttering vowel: shewa.
44. /ə/ *drama, item, devil, button, circus*

25 Consonants + 19 Vowels = 44 Speech Sounds spelled with 23 Letters

This *Foundation for Phonics Chart* was developed by Donald L. Potter from Dr. Rudolf Flesch's discussion, "What is Phonics?" in *Why Johnny Can't Read and what you can do about It*. This chart was prepared on 9/22/04 and published on the Internet on 11/3/04. The *72 Exercises* Dr. Flesch developed for teaching students to read the 44 speech sounds using the 26 letters of the alphabet can be found in the last half of his book. Other information on phonics reading instruction can be found on the *Education Page* of my website: www.donpotter.net.

Two Difficulties of Our Alphabet System and Our System of Spelling:

1. We have half as many letters as we have sounds – which means that half the symbols a child has to learn consist not of one letter but two – like *ay, ea, sh, ch,* and so on.
2. Our most important single letters are used to spell two or more entirely different sounds, namely, the five vowels, *a, e, i, o, u,* and the consonants *c* and *g*.

Therefore,

if you want to teach a child to read without utterly confusing him, you have to start with single letters that stand for single sounds, then go on to sounds spelled by two-letter or three-letter combinations, and finally teach him that some letters do not spell one sound but two.

The Catch:

You can't teach a child to read without letting him read words. And every word in English has a vowel. So you *have* to start with teaching the child the letters *a, e, i, o, u* in spite of the fact that each of them spells a long *and* a short vowel. The only way to solve this problem is to begin by teaching the child only the five *short* vowels (which are far more common than the long ones) and postpone the long vowels until a much later stage.

The Natural Sequence of *any* phonics method is:

Step One: The five short vowels and all consonant combinations spelled by a single letter.

Step Two: Consonants and consonant combinations spelled with two or three letters.

Step Three: The five long vowels: v-c-e: (mate, mete, mite, mote, mute)

Step Four: R-Controlled Vowels (c<u>ar</u>, f<u>or</u>k, f<u>ur</u>/f<u>ir</u>/h<u>er</u>/doct<u>or</u>)

Step Five: Vowels and vowel combinations spelled with two or three letters.

Step Six: Irregular Spellings.

This information on phonics was extracted from pages 27 through 32 of Rudolf Flesch's 1955 *Why Johnny Can't Read and what you can do about it*. The Five Steps here are based on the Scope & Sequence of Hazel Logan Loring's 1980 *Reading Made Easy with Blend Phonics for First Grade*. Dr. Flesch taught the vowel combinations (also called: vowel teams, or digraphs & diphthongs) before the long-vowel VCE pattern. Flesch had only four steps because he included the r-controlled vowels with vowel combinations (digraphs and diphthongs).

Blend Phonics Timed Fluency Drills
Sound-to-Symbol Skills & Drills Coalition

Step	Unit	Association	Drills
Step 6 Advanced Spellings & Open Syllables	--	3 & 4 Syllable Words	61
	47	37 Dolch List Words and 3 /zh/ words	60
	46	Long Vowels in Open syllables	59,
	45	ed with short e; ed sounds like 'd; ed sounds like 't	57, 58 Suffixes
	44	Final le, tion, sion	56
	43	ph sounds like f	55
	42	se sounds like z	54
	41	Silent k, w, t, b, l. and h	53
	40	Silent gh, and gh like f	52
	39	Soft sound of g in dge & sometimes before e, i, y.	51
	38	Soft sound of c (before e, i, & y); s like sh (sugar)	50
	37	Phonograms: ul, ull, ush (u sound like short oo)	49
	36	Unaccented a at beginning of words & a	48
Step 5 Vowel Digraphs & Diphthongs	35	Diagraphs ew, ue	47
	34	Phonograms: al, all	46
	33	Vowel Digraphs aw, au	45
	32	Short sound of oo	43, 44 Mixed oo
	31	Long sound of oo	42
	30	Diphthong: oy, oi	40, 41 Mix
	29	Diphthong ou; Digraph ōu, often Irregular	39
	28	Digraph: ōw, Diphthong: ow	38
	27	Vowel Digraph: oa, oe (like long ō)	37
	26	Final Vowel y (ē); Long ī in single syllable words	36
	25	Vowel Digraph ie (long ī and long ē)	35
	24	Vowel Digraph ea (long ē, short ĕ, long ā)	34
	23	Vowel Digraph: ee	33
	22	Vowel Digraph: ai, ay	32
Step 4 R-Contr. Vowels	21	Phonogram er, ir, ur, and sometimes or	29, 30, 31 Review
	20	Phonogram: or	28
	19	Phonogram: ar	26
Step 3 Long Vowels (VCE)	18	Short words ending in long vowels: be, go, he, me, etc.	25, 26 Rev.
	17	Phonograms - Long Vowels: old, olt, oll, ost,, oth, ild, ind	
	16	VCE (long vowels)	18, 19, 20, 21, 22, 23, 25
Step 2 Consonant Blends & Digraphs & Compound Words	15	Short Vowel Compound Words	17
	14	Initial Consonant Blends: br, cr, dr, fr, gr, pr, tr	15, 16
	13	Initial Consonant Blends: bl, cl, fl, gl, pl, sc, sk, sm, sl, sn, sp, st, sw	13, 14
	12	nk (ank, ink, onk, unk)	12
	11	ng (ang, ing, ong, ung)	
	10	Consonant Digraph: wh	
	9	Consonant Digraphs: ch, tch (ch = k)	11
	8	Consonant Digraphs: th (voiced); *th* (unvoiced)	
	7	Consonant Digraph: sh	
	6	Final Consonant Blends	10
Step 1 Short Vowels & Consonants	5	Short vowel ĕ	8, 9
	4	Short vowel ŭ	6, 7
	3	Short vowel ŏ	4, 5
	2	Short vowel ĭ	2, 3
	1	Short vowel ă b c d f g h j k l m n p qu r s t v w y z ck	1

74

Blend Phonics Timed Fluency Drills
Student Progress Chart

Name: _____ Grade: _____ Teacher: _____ Goal_____

Step 1 Short Vowels & Consonants	Step 2 Consonant Blends & Digraphs	Step 3 Long Vowels v-e	Step 4 R-Controlled Vowels	Step 5 Vowel Digraphs & Diphthongs	Step 6 Irregular Spellings
Drill 1 ă	Drill 10 End Blends	Drill 18 a-e	Drill 27 ar	Drill 32 ay/ai	Drill 48 Beg. unacc. a=ū
Drill 2 ĭ	Drill 11 Cons. Digraphs	Drill 19 e-e i-e	Drill 28 or	Drill 33 ēe/ēa	Drill 49 u =Short oo
Drill 3 ă ĭ	Drill 12 -ng – kn	Drill 20 ā ē ī	Drill 29 er, ir, ur, or	Drill 34 ĕa, eā	Drill 50 Soft c /s/
Drill 4 ŏ	Drill 13 Beg. Cons. Blends 1	Drill 21 o-e	Drill 30 R-Cont. Vowels	Drill 35 īe, iē	Drill 51 Soft g /j/
Drill 5 ă, ĭ, ŏ	Drill 14 Beg. Cons. Blends 2	Drill 22 ā ē ī ō	Drill 31 Review Steps 1-4	Drill 36 Final -ȳ --y=ē	Drill 52 gh=f & silent gh
Drill 6 ŭ	Drill 15 Beg. Cons. Blends 3	Drill 23 u-e		Drill 37 oa/oe	Drill 53 Silent k w t b l
Drill 7 ă ĭ ŏ ŭ	Drill 16 Beg. Cons. Blends 4	Drill 24 ā ē ī ō ū		Drill 38 ōw: rose, ow: cow	Drill 54 s = z
Drill 8 ĕ	Drill 17 2-syl. words	Drill 25 LV Phonograms		Drill 39 ou/ow: <u>cow</u>	Drill 55 ph = /f/ ; gh = f
Drill 9 ă ĭ ŏ ŭ ĕ		Drill 26 SV/LV Rev.		Drill 40 oi/oy	Drill 56 -le; tion/sion = sh
				Drill 41 Digrah/Diph. Mix	Drill 57 ed = ĕd, d, t
				Drill 42 Long oo	Drill 58 -y, -ier, -ies.- ily
				Drill 43 Short oo	Drill 59 LV Open Syll.
				Drill 44 oo Mixed	Drill 60 37 Dolch, zh
				Drill 45 aw/au/a(l)	Drill 61 3 & 4 Syll. Words
				Drill 46 ew/ue	
				Drill 47 aw/au/a(l), ew/ue	

BLEND PHONICS TIMED DECODING FLUENCY RECORD SHEET

Name: _____ Grade/Age: _____ Teacher _____ Goal ____

Drill	Words Per Minute			Average	Date	Signature
	1st Timing	2nd Timing	3rd Timing			

Notes Concerning the History and Development
of the *Blend Phonics Timed Fluency Drills*

By Donald L. Potter

On January 5, 1998, I called Mr. August C. Enderlin III, the author of the 1970 *Victory Drill Book: A phonetic approach to reading with an emphasis on speed.* Mr. Enderlin explained to me how he developed the VDB. He worked for a school in the Midwest that used Rudolf Flesch's 72 Exercises as their main phonics program. Flesch's book went out of print so they reprinted it with sentences for the Review Lessons and added Rules in the back of the book. He confirmed that the VDB was a single-letter phonics program. I corresponded with Mr. Enderlin via email on March 25, 2000 to let him know that one of my students had make great progress with the VDB. I had ordered a copy and used it in some of my tutoring. It was on March 11, 2003 that I called Mr. Edward Miller concerning his *Miller Word Identification Assessment* for artificially induced whole-word dyslexia. Mr. Miller told me that he used Rudolf Flesch's 72 Exercises to cure this common form of dyslexia caused by faulty classroom reading instruction that emphasized sight-word memorization and context guessing. I spent the next few months reading and rereading Flesch's 1955 *Why Johnny Can't Read and what you can do about it.* I discovered that Flesch used what was known as single-letter phonics as contrasted with word-family (or spelling family) phonics. Flesch also explained in detailed prose the linguistics behind his phonics method, which is the same as that behind all real phonics methods of teaching reading. Shortly thereafter, I published on my website, the results of my painstaking linguistic research into Dr. Flesch's method.

I had hoped to get some of the VDB schools to give Mr. Miller's MWIA to all their students so we could get longitudinal scores on the impact of the VDB Drills; and because of their virtual identity, Flesch's 72 Exercises. Mr. Enderlin later graciously sent me the names and address of the schools that used the VDB, but I was never able to make further headway with my research project. I think it would have proven beyond a shadow of a doubt that students who learned to read with Flesch's 72 Exercises (and the VDB high speed phonics technique) were totally free of any artificially induced whole-word dyslexia. I would still like to see that research conducted.

In 2009 Andrea Cartensen extensively revised the VDB, but retained the idea of timing students and the other main features of the program. The new book changed the sequence, but maintained the scope of the program. The 1970 VDB was practically identical to the Rudolf Flesch's 72 Exercises in his 1955 *Why Johnny Can't Read*. The new program reorders the material a bit, but accomplishes the same purposes. The website for the new book is www.victorydrillbook.com

The key to the *Blend Phonics Timed Fluency Drills* is the list of words strategically grouped together by spelling patterns. As the patterns are mastered, students become progressively better prepared for paragraph reading. In the process, an emphasis on speed enhances the essential transition from "sounding out" to efficient reading. This is the exact OPPOSITE of the all-too-common Sight Word drills.

Because the high-speed phonics method allows each child to progress at his or her own rate, the *Blend Phonics Timed Fluency Drills* works as well for the beginner as it does for the older struggling reader. As students finish each page at the minimum speed calibrated for the appropriate grade level, they move on to the next drill, where new sound-to-symbol correspondences are mastered for rapid and accurate response to each word.

By the time a beginning or remedial student can pass Drill 47 at a minimum of 40 wpm, they can be considered a "free reader," able to read anything on their grade level.

The students like to color the squares for the drill on the Student Progress Chart once they are able to read at the calibrated speed for their grade level. Sometimes it is better let them pass at a lower than calibrated speed to keep them from getting discouraged, but going through the program again at higher speeds until they can reach their calibrated speed.

I would like to acknowledge the encouragement and help from Kathy Alfke, a highly experienced reading teacher in Indiana. She has many years experience timing students with the old and new editions of the VDB. Her help has been of inestimable value.

This document was last revised on October 11, 2017.

Special Note Concerning "Total Recall of the Alphabet:"

June Brown in her excellent 1981 *Guide to Let's Read*, says,

> Every child I worked with learned to read providing he or she could see a pin on the floor and pick it up, could button clothes, and *had total recall of the alphabet.* No one can read an alphabet language without total recall of the alphabet. 'Total recall' means that the student can recite the letters in alphabetical order, can identify them when they are presented in random order, and can print any word when it is pronounced and spelled. These three goals must be met with absolute perfection before the student can become a good reader. Unfortunately, many schools do not insist on total recall. They teach children to recite the letters in alphabetical order, and sometimes they teach them to identify the letters in random order. However, very few schools teach children to print any word when it is pronounced and spelled. The foundation of reading success is total recall of the alphabet. (7)

Concerning dyslexia, June Brown had some interesting comments:

> Let's get the facts straight! There is no such thing as dyslexia among children who know the alphabet. Any child who can learn the alphabet is not dyslexic. Therefore, if your child knows the alphabet, can see normally, can button clothes, your child can and will learn to read. "Dyslexia" is a very confusing term. Many educators no longer use it because no one is quite sure what it means. Generally it means that a child can only read with great difficulty, but sometimes it means a child cannot read at all. I have seen many children labeled dyslexic. But every one of them who knew the alphabet learned to read. (12)

Marilyn Jager Adams wrote in her 1990 *Beginning to Reading: Thinking and Learning about Print*,

> Both theory and data suggest that instruction on neither the sounds of letters nor the recognition of whole words should be earnestly undertaken until the child has become confident and quick at recognizing individual letters (363).

The following observations are from Marilyn Jager Adams' 2013 *ABC Foundations for Young Children: A Classroom Curriculum.*

> Children need to know the alphabet. To use phonemic awareness for reading, children need to know which letter represents which phoneme. In turn, learning letter-sound correspondences requires that children not only be able to discern each letter but also to identify each letter by shape, confidently and securely. To use their phonemic awareness to write, children must also be able to form the letters with legible accuracy and reasonable ease. For much of their classroom instruction on reading and spelling, they must be able not only to recognize each letter, but also to seek, recall, or even image the letter given only its name or sound. (2).

> Even so, the issue is deeper than that, for children's letter knowledge is a good predictor of their responsiveness to phonemic training. ... It may well be, as several have argued, that gaining phonemics awareness *depends* on prior letter knowledge. (2)

> Studies commonly show that only a minority of children are able to name or write all letters of the alphabet by the end of first grade and that the number who know the letter sounds is still smaller. (2)

> Leading children to practice a consistent set of strokes for each letter serves to accelerate the development of letter-writing automaticity. Furthermore, as the hand movements involved in writing each letters becomes bound to the visual representation, they serve to hasten and secure the child's ability to recognize the letters. (59)

Alphabet Letter Recognition Test

Name: _____ Date: _____ Age _____ Grade _____

School _____ Uppercase LPM ____ Lowercase LPM _____

Uppercase Manuscript

I E A Z W S O K G C X

T P L H D U Q M Y V R

N J F B

Lowercase Manuscript

u p m y v r n j f b x t p i

h d l e a z w s o k g c

Direction: Time how long it takes the students to identify the letters and divide 1560 by the time in seconds to get the letters-per-minute (LPM). LPM=1560/time-in-seconds. Use the same formula to determine alphabet writing fluency.

TAP THE ALPHABET FOR FLUENCY
MANUSCRIPT LOWERCASE

a   b   c   d

e   f   g

h   i   j   k

l   m   n   o   p

q   r   s

t   u   v

w   x   y   z

TAP THE ALPHABET FOR FLUENCY

Manuscript Uppercase

A   B   C   D

E   F   G

H   I   J   K

L   M   N   O   P

Q   R   S

T   U   V

W   X   Y   Z

Phonovisual Phoneme Fluency Probe: Consonants

p   b   m
                     mb

wh   w   qu

f   v
ph gh

th   th

t   d   n   l
                     kn gn   le

s   z   r
c   se   wr

sh   y
ti si ci

ch   j
  tch   g

k   g   ng   x
c ck   n(k)

h

Phonovisual Phoneme Fluency Probe: Vowels

a-e	ee	i-e	o-e	u-e
ay ai ea^3 eigh	-e ea^1 ie	-y igh	oa ow^2 -o	ew ue

-a-	-e-	-i-	-o-	-u-
	ea^2	-y	wa-	o^3

aw

au a(ll)

oo

ur

er ir or^2

a(r)

oo

u^3

ow

ou

oy

oi

o(r)

Students should be able to identify by sound all 43 sound-to-symbol relationships by the end of kindergarten. Students should be able to say 50—60 phonemes (speech sounds) per minute. Flashcards with and without the pictures clues should be used to develop and test fluency. Order Phonovisual Charts from www.phonovisual.com

consonants

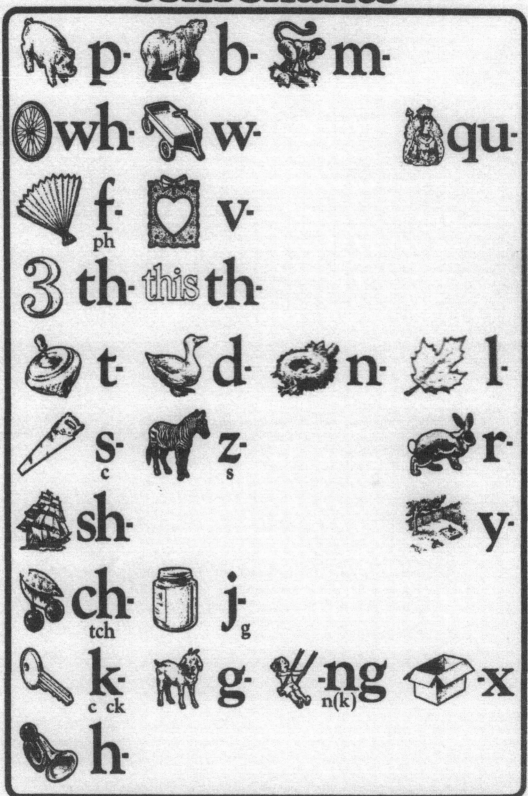

vowels

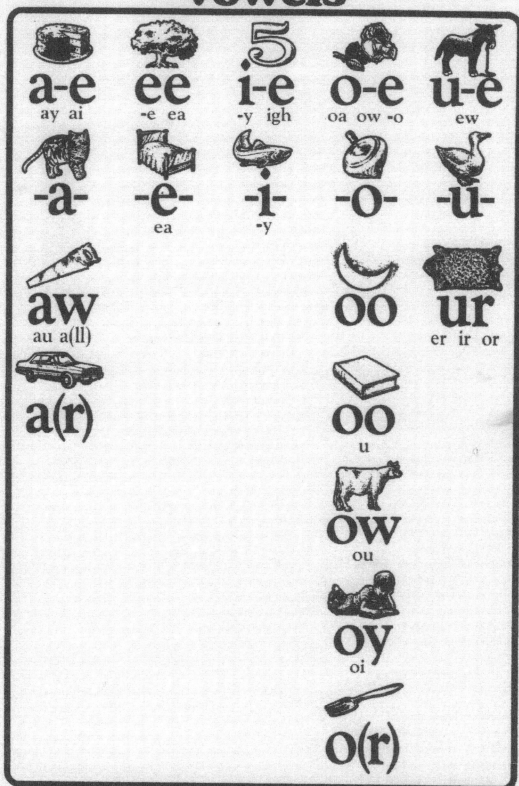

Information on Fluency
from
The Morningside Model of Generative Instruction

Dr. Bob Rose brought the *Morningside Model of Instruction* to my attention in his thought-provoking book, *FORGET THE BELL CURVE*. In June 2011, I got a copy of Ken Johnson's and Elizabeth M. Street's book, *THE MORNINGSIDE MODEL OF GENERATIVE INSTRUCTION: WHAT IT MEANS TO LEAVE NO CHILD BEHIND*, CAMBRIDGE CENTER FOR BEHAVIORAL STUDIES, 2004.

I simply want to show insights that I gained from the book that relate to the nature of fluency as it relates to the development of alphabet letter writing and identification fluency and word decoding fluency (word identification). I have two main points: 1) to show that insufficient fluency does not support student advancement in the same way that higher levels of fluency do, and 2) to encourage teachers to help students achieve the necessary levels of fluency through well designed daily practice drills.

In the following paragraphs, I will present information from *The Morningside Model of Generative Instruction* as a series of quotations with comments. My comments are in [brackets].

The elegance of an instructional program depends on the programmer's ability to detect and teach some minimal response or generative set which can combine and recombine into the universal set of all possible relationships. One is looking, very simply, for the exponential value of key instructional events, in which behaviors that emerge are in a power relationship to the elements which are taught (28f). [Generative is also called "contingency adduction," in which the contingency "draws out" the additional (novel) behavior. Learning the alphabet to fluency is a "key instructional event" which has a "power relationship" (possessing exponential value) with learning to read and spell. The paragraph goes on to illustrate by comparing sight-word and phonics instruction. Sight Word instruction possesses no power-relationship (exponential value) to reading because it does not generalize to other words, phonics, on the other hand, "will reliably produce recombinative reading behavior, guaranteeing successful reading of thousands of words beyond those taught in the original instruction."]

The goal of fluency building is to build hardy academic behaviors – behaviors that weather periods of no practice, occur with short latencies, are impervious to distraction, and are easily accessible in new situations (30).

Precision Teaching was conceived by Dr. Ogden Lindsey at the University of Kansas in his quest for a mechanism that brought continuous measurement and rate data into educational practice. Lindsey was heavily influenced by Skinner's allegiance to **rate** as the primary datum for studying behavioral change, and he recognized that traditional educational measurement systems that depend on percent correct and letter grades placed artificial ceilings on performance and lead students and teachers to a false security about the strength of their performance. Both Skinner and Lindsey believed that **high-rate behavior** not only looked different than low-rate behavior, it also **had fundamentally different features** (66).

In Precision Teaching parlance, once a performance demonstrates retention, endurance, and application, it is *fluent*. As a metaphor, performance fluency is flowing, flexible, effortless, errorless, automatic, confident, second nature and masterful. When performance is fluent, it becomes a highly probable activity. Fluent performance is fun, energetic, naturally reinforced behavior. Dr. Carl Binder coined the term *fluency building* to refer to practice activities that are designed to achieve these goals. [My *Alphabet Fluency Tapping Exercises* and *Blend Phonics Timed Fluency Drills* are designed with this purpose in mind. Fluency Building is also called Frequency Building.] Currently at Morningside, we use five characteristics of performance to set fluency performance frequencies, changing the acronym to RESAA: **R**etention, **E**ndurance, **S**tability, **A**pplication, and **A**dduction (67).

Dr. Robert Gangé on Automaticity

From "Mastery Learning and Instructional Design," *Performance Improvement Quarterly*, 1988.

Intellectual skills that are highly practiced come to be performed automatically, that is, they demand little conscious attention. The skilled student of geometry doesn't have to "stop and think" about how to find the value of the complementary angle of 100 degrees – instead, its value of 80 degrees is known automatically once its direction and origin are perceived. The skilled reader does not slow down his comprehension in order to pay conscious attention to the difference between *welcome* and *winsome*, because the differences in their sounds are automatically processed. The skilled writer doesn't stop to attend to the form of a past participle of the word *go*, but writes automatically, "I have gone."

By definition a skill becomes automatic when it can be performed without interfering with a second simultaneous task. In practice, automaticity is achieved by repeated performances in different examples. For instruction, one of the best procedures appears to be involving learners in game-like exercises in which they strive to beat their previous times in performance of a skill.

The main importance of automatization of skills lies in the freeing of attention for other tasks, particularly those that involve problem solving. Thus, reading comprehension depends on the automatization of decoding skills, so that the "thinking" part of reading can be done. The solving of arithmetic word problems depends on the automatization of skills in mathematical translation in order that attention be made available for problem solving activity. Skillful automobile driving likewise requires the presence of automatized component skills of acceleration, braking, and steering. Here is the way I would state the most important hypothesis in this area:

> The *principal factor* affecting the development of higher level thinking in learners is the release of attention by automatization of basic skills.

In his 1981 book, *Why Johnny STILL Can't Read and what you can do about it*, Rudolf Flesch tells us, "I wrote to Dr. Gagné and asked him how he first developed his ideas. He answered:

> My ideas about task analysis, learning hierarchies and subordinate skills came originally from a study I did on the learning of ninth graders in a mathematics problem (inferring and stating a general formula for the sum of terms in a number series.) When I ran across some students who seemed to be having particular difficulties learning to perform this task, it seemed go me they were missing some "subordinate skills," in some cases rather simple arithmetic skills. Accordingly, I did a study in which I first analyzed the subordinate skills of the number-series task, then tested students on them, and taught them the subordinate skills they didn't' know. As a research psychologist used to the notion that learning is a gradual process. I was surprised at the results. Once subordinate skills were mastered, the new learning was very rapid, and "sudden." (35)

In the same book, Dr. Flesch quotes Drs. Isabelle Y. Liberman and Donald Shankweilder of the University of Connecticut:

> Instructional procedures inform children early on that the printed word of the component phonemes [sounds] and their particular succession in the spoken word.... The instruction should not, as it often does, mislead children into assuming that the printed word is an ideographic symbol, a notion that will have to be corrected later and, apparently for some children, with great difficulty. Procedures that initiate children into the mystique of reading by drawing their attention to the visual configuration ("remember the shape 'tail'") and its associated meaning ("the one with the tail means monkey") without alerting them to the relevance of the sound structure of the word may lead them into a blind alley. Their ability to memorize shapes and associated meanings of a handful of words may lull them and their parents into the comfortable belief that they can read, but it may leave them stranded at that state, functional illiterates with no keys to unlock new words. (38). Emphasis by Donald L. Potter.

DIRECTIONS

for the *MILLER WORD IDENTIFICATION ASSESSMENT I* (MWIA I)

Charles M. Richardson, B.S, M.S, P.E, September 25, 2003
Revised by Donald L. Potter June 10, 2016

INTRODUCTION

The MWIA Level I is a quick way to see how a person analyzes words: By decoding (sounding-out), by sight memorization, or a mix of the two. The MWIA consists of a "Holistic" and a "Phonetic" list. You need a pen/pencil, stopwatch or equivalent, a clipboard or folder to hold your copy out of sight of the student, and a copy of the test for the student. (Use a separate copy to record each student's responses.) If the student is apprehensive about being timed, tell him this is part of some research (which it is) and that we need to see if he reads one list slower or faster than the other. Explain that he should read aloud across each line (point), and stop at the end of the first list.

TESTING

When you and your watch are ready, tell him to begin, and start your watch. Underline each word he mis-calls, but give no hint or signal; if he self-corrects, just circle the word. If possible, mark some indication of his error for later analysis. When he completes the Holistic list, stop your watch. Ask him to wait while you record the time, and reset your watch.

Repeat as above for the next list. Stop your watch; record the time.

On the PHONETIC LIST ONLY, re-visit all of the words he mis-called, point to each and say, "Spell this out loud while you're looking at it, then say it again." If he says it right, complete the underline into a full circle around the word. If he still says it wrong, bracket the word /thus/ to indicate that it was attempted but not successful. If he "blurts out" the correct word without spelling it, just circle the word. Enter the # of words spell-corrected and total # re-tried for the Phonetic list.

SCORING

Convert the recorded times to speeds in WPM (words-per-minute) by the formula (3000 divided by seconds). Record WPM's. The percent slow-down (SD) from the Holistic speed (HS) to the Phonetic speed (PS) is 100(PS/HS) subtracted from 100: 100 - 100(PS/HS) = %SD

INTERPRETATION

Severity of "Whole-Word-Dyslexia" (WWD) is proportional to %SD and the rise in errors on the Phonetic list. Up to 5% SD is mild, 10-20% is moderate, >20% is severe. Up to 3 Phonetic errors is mild, 4-8 is moderate, >10 is severe. Combinations are left to the judgment of the examiner. Examine the errors: if the substituted word is a "look-alike," he's using memory instead of decoding. If he switches a vowel, it's a phonetic error. If he mistakes look-alike consonants, e.g., "n" or "b" for an "h," it could signal a visual difficulty. The above are not absolutes!

The Miller Word-Identification Assessment I

SUMMARY SHEET

Donald L. Potter, June 10, 2016

Name _____ M (__)/F (__) Age ____ Grade ____ Test Date _____

School _____ City/State _____

Level I

Holistic WPM _____ Phonetic WPM _____ Difference _____

Difference _____/Holistic WPM _____ x 100 = _____% of Slow-down

Holistic Errors ____ Phonetic Errors ____ Difference ____

Ratio of Phonic Errors _____/Holistic errors _____ = _____

Phonetic Corrected ____ out of ____ attempted.

Tested by _____

Scored by _____

K – 1 School _____ City/State/District _____

Method/Program _____

Publisher _____

Comments:

Miller Word Identification Assessment - Level 1

Name _____ M (__)/F(__) Age ___ Grade ___ Test Date _____

<u>Holistic</u>   Time ___:___" = (_____ Sec)\3000 = _____ WPM Errors _____

the	to	and	a	I	you	it	in
said	for	up	look	is	go	we	little
down	can	see	not	one	my	me	big
come	blue	red	where	jump	away	here	help
make	yellow	two	play	run	find	three	funny
he	was	that	she	on	they	but	at
with	all						

<u>Phonetic</u> Time ___'___" = (___Sec)\3000 = _____ WPM Errors ____

Spell-Correct ___/_____   Slow-Down _____%

bib	nip	map	tag	job	met	sip	mix
pad	lock	wig	pass	hot	rack	jet	kid
pack	Tom	luck	neck	pick	cut	deck	kick
duck	fuzz	mud	hack	sick	men	hunt	rash
pest	land	tank	rush	mash	rest	tent	fond
bulk	dust	desk	wax	ask	gulps	ponds	hump
lamp	belt						

Advice for Remedial Reading Teachers

From Dr. Rudolf Flesch

"To begin with, let's try **to isolate Johnny from his word-guessing environment**. While he is in school, that is difficult or almost impossible. So the best thing will be to work with him during the summer vacations. Let him **stop all reading** – all *attempts* to read. Explain to him that now he is going to learn to how to read, and that for the time being, books are out. All he'll get for several months are lessons in phonics. … This, incidentally, is important. Take him fully into your confidence and explain to him exactly what you are trying to do. Tell him that you are going to do something **new** with him – something entirely different from what his teachers did in school. Tell him that this is *certain* to work. Convince him that as soon as he has taken this medicine he will be cured. … Start him on the phonics lessons. Go with him through the Exercises, one by one, always making sure that he has mastered the previous one before you go on to the next. …**Only when you are through – or almost through – with the drills and exercises, start him again on reading**. At first, let him read aloud to you. Watch like a hawk that he doesn't guess a single word. Interrupt him every time he does it and let him work out the word phonetically. He'll never learn to read if he doesn't get over the word-guessing habit" (*Why Johnny Can't Read*, 115).

"Use the exercises to teach writing and spelling as well as reading. You will probably be tempted to go ahead with the reading and slight the writing and spelling. Try to resist temptation. Ideally, Johnny should learn to read and write each word at the same time. Let him write each word from dictation. It is well worth taking the extra time. (140)

"There is a large amount of repetition in the exercises… However, that doesn't mean that doing each exercise once is enough. Do each of them until Johnny can read and write each word in it without the slightest hesitation. When you have done all the words horizontally, from left to right do them vertically. Do them from right to left. Do them from the bottom up, diagonally, and pick words here and there at random. Make sure as you can that Johnny can really read all the words. (140)

"If you use phonics as *the* method of teaching reading, you teach children the alphabet code. You do this step by step, in easy stages. At each step, you give the children plenty of material to practice on. When you teach them the short *o*, you give them a hundred words or more with short *o* to read aloud again and again until the pronunciation of the short *o* has become **fully automatic**. You do the same thing with short *u* and *ch* and *th* and *igh* and *ou* and *mps* – through the whole inventory of 181 items until it's all **firmly fixed in the pupil's subconscious mind**. Sounding out and blending practicing – there is no other way. It's like practicing scales on the piano or practicing driving until you're good enough for the road test" (*Why Johnny Still Can't Read*, 75).

Summary of Scientific Research

Notes from Keith Stanovitch's *Progress in Understanding Reading*

Whole Language advocates such as Ken Goodman and Frank Smith hold that the skilled reader is less reliant on graphic clues and more reliant on contextual information than is the less-skilled reader. Scientific research conduct by Keith Sandovich and Rich West set out to verify the Whole Language thesis. To their surprise, all of their research pointed in the opposite direction; it was the poorer readers, not the more skilled readers, who were more reliant on context to facilitate word recognition. Following LaBerge and Samuels, they came to realize that skilled readers develop fluency by automating certain low-level processes such as letter and word recognition so that the students limited attention capacity can be allocated to higher-level functions such as comprehension. A process is considered to be automated when it can take place without attention being directed to it. The capacity freed by automatic word recognition processes becomes available for various comprehension strategies. The goal of the *Blend Phonics Fluency Drills* is to automate lower-level word recognition so that cognitive capacity can be freed up and made available for higher-level comprehension tasks.

On the Use of the Decoding Proficiency Graph

Research indicates that automaticity of decoding skills facilitates reading comprehension and is often a prerequisite to the more complex comprehension skills of reasoning and inference. Students' skills must be automatic (proficient) before they can comprehend passages or progress to more difficult skills. Thus, once students have demonstrated that they can read the words in a *Blend Phonics Timed Fluency Drill* untimed with 90 percent accuracy, they should work on increasing their reading speed by doing frequent rate timings. The Decoding Proficiency Graphs are optional. They are included for teachers who want to plot skill development.

Use a timer to time students as they read the Drill for one minute. A warm-up timing can be used for practice before doing a second, official, timing. If students finish the Drill in less than a minute, they should return to the beginning and continue to read until the time is up. Progress is then recorded on the Decoding Proficiency Graph, indicating the number of words read correctly in a minute as well as the number of errors. The goal will follow the "Blend Phonics Minimum Oral Reading Speeds." Below is a sample graph to illustrate the process. Recording errors is an option. I generally just have the student correct any errors as they read: the slow-down serves as an index of errors without the need to count them.

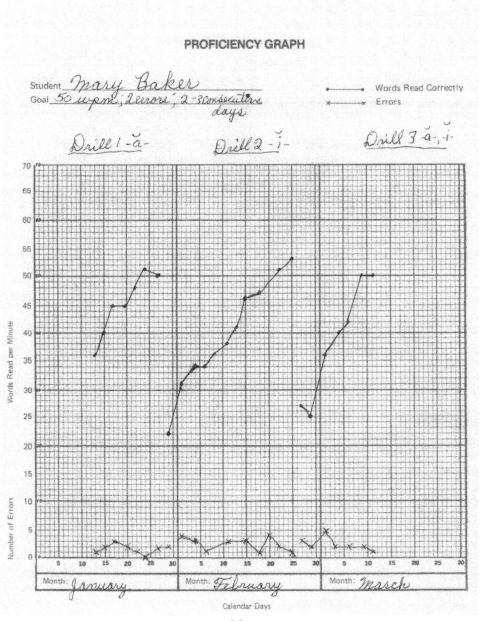

92

PROFICIENCY GRAPH

Student _____

Goal _____

●————● Words Read Correctly

×————× Errors

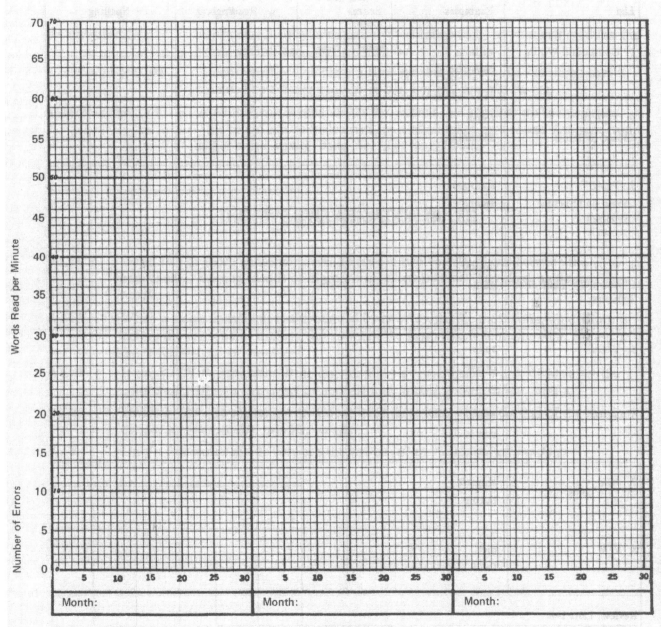

Calendar Days

About the Author

Mr. Donald L. Potter has been teaching beginning and remedial reading for nearly thirty years. He subbed full time for all subjects and grade levels for five years before becoming a certified teacher. He was a public school teacher for the Ector County ISD in Odessa Texas for twenty-one years, teaching elementary bilingual, secondary Spanish, Amateur Radio (NG5W), and dyslexia classes.

Mr. Potter currently teaches Spanish, remedial reading, and cursive handwriting at the Odessa Christian School in Odessa, TX. In the evenings after school, and during summer vacation, he tutors students of all ages who have reading problems.

He has been publishing on the Internet since 2003. His website, www.donpotter.net, is a rich resource for educators looking for workable solutions to reducing the high illiteracy rates in America and other English speaking countries. .

He is the sponsor of *The Blend Phonics Nationwide Educational Reform Campaign* at www.blendphonics.org. This Campaign is based on the highly effective *Blend Phonics* approach published by Mrs. Hazel Logan Loring in 1980. Thousand of teachers have found this to be one of the most effective and easiest-to-teach methods ever published.

He is an experienced handwriting teacher. His *Shortcut to Manuscript* and *Shortcut to Cursive* are available for free from his website. He has used both systems successful with students from kindergarten through adult. Fluent handwriting (writing rapidly and legibly) is a **necessary foundation** for fluent reading and accurate spelling.

Mr. Potter has published several books on teaching reading:

1. Hazel Loring's 1980 *Reading Made Easy with Blend Phonics for First Grade, Plus Fluency Drills*
2. Donald Potter with Elizabeth Brown 2015 *Blend Phonics Lessons and Stories*
3. *Blend Phonics Timed Fluency Drills* (2016)
4. Florence Akin's 1913 *Word Mastery: Phonics for the First Three Grades*
5. Samuel L Blumenfeld's *First Readers Anthology.*
6. *Noah Webster's Spelling Book Method for Teaching Reading and Spelling.*
7. Margaret Haliburton 1906 *Playmates Primer: A First Reader for Boys and Girls*

Made in the USA
San Bernardino, CA
23 March 2018